THE POETRY OF CHILDHOOD

The Artist's Children. *August Edouart*

The
Poetry of
Childhood

edited by Samuel Carr

B.T. Batsford Ltd, London

ISBN 0 7134 3445 7

Phototypeset in 12 on 13pt. Bembo by Servis Filmsetting Ltd, Manchester and printed in Great Britain by Butler & Tanner Ltd, Frome, Somerset

for the publishers, B.T. Batsford Ltd, 4 Fitzhardinge Street, London W1H 0AH

Contents

The Illustrations

The paintings reproduced on the endpapers, 'The Smile' and 'The Frown', are by Thomas Webster (1800–1886). *The Guildhall Art Gallery, London*

Thomas Bewick

Introduction

Childhood! happiest stage of life,
Free from care and free from strife,
Free from Memory's ruthless reign,
Fraught with scenes of former pain;
Free from Fancy's cruel skill,
Fabricating future ill;
Time when all that meets the view,
All can charm, for all is new.

That is one view of childhood. Another, contrasting one (from a play of Beaumont and Fletcher's) asks:

What benefit can children be
But charges and disobedience? What's the
Love they render at one and twenty years?
. . . When they are young, they
Are like bells rung backwards, nothing but noise
And giddiness.

There is little doubt, I suppose, that the first quotation (from the minor eighteenth-century poet, John Scott) is not only feebler poetry but also farther removed from the truth about its subject.

The fact is that children are both endearing and egocentric, beautiful in themselves and sometimes ugly in their behaviour. That they are so should come as no surprise: their lovableness and their egocentricity are alike the means by which they are enabled to survive. It is natural that the most prolific writers for and about children have seldom had sons or daughters of their own. On the contrary, like Blake and Christina Rossetti, Lear and Lewis Carroll, Charles and Mary Lamb, Isaac Watts and Cowper, R.L. Stevenson and Beatrix Potter, they have more often been childless. Only writers whose experience of children was as it were at one remove have been able to overlook the reality and to romanticise it.

9

Few poets have described experience from a child's point of view. Clare and Cowper and Wordsworth on occasion did so, but it is more common to find the poet commenting on some aspect of childhood from an adult's standpoint. The proportion of poems concerned with the first year or two of a child's life greatly exceeds those devoted to the succeeding period. Nor is there any lack of poems about the sad and premature mortality of children. The reason is the same one. The later years of childhood have not on the whole been found suitable themes for poetry. Poets have preferred to write of children young enough to be imagined as they are not.

For the artist the child is generally regarded more objectively, as a shape to be recorded. Once let emotion enter in and with it too often comes the falsification of a Millais or a Kate Greenaway. Rembrandt and Frans Hals, Millet and Courbet, by contrast, saw children as they were. In spite of a consequent degree of coarseness, even brutality, in the treatment there nonetheless resulted some of the finest pictures of children that have been painted. At the other extreme, Renoir and Gainsborough were exceptional in their ability to make fine pictures out of undeniably pretty children.

Since the poems in this collection are English (or American) the illustrations have for the most part been taken from the work of English artists. There has perhaps been some loss here since English painting is in a class inferior to English poetry. Still, it was thought that the complement would be closer, and as the subject of childhood has generally been more attractive to artists than to poets, the range of choice has still been wide.

Ages of Childhood
from: As You Like It

At first the Infant,
Mewling, and puking in the Nurse's armes:
Then, the whining Schoole-boy with his Satchell
And shining morning face, creeping like snaile
Unwillingly to schoole.

WILLIAM SHAKESPEARE (1564–1616)

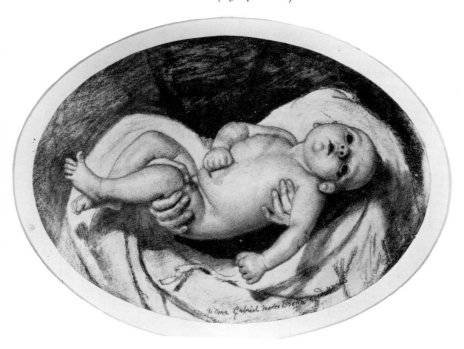

The Artist's Son. Ford Madox Brown

On Visiting the Grave of my Stillborn Little Girl

Sunday, July 4th, 1836

I made a vow within my soul, O child,
When thou wert laid beside my weary heart,
With marks of death on every tender part,
That, if in time a living infant smiled,
Winning my ear with gentle sounds of love
In sunshine of such joy, I still would save
A green rest for thy memory, O Dove!
And oft times visit thy small, nameless grave.
Thee have I not forgot, my firstborn, thou
Whose eyes ne'er opened to my wistful gaze,
Whose sufferings stamped with pain thy little brow;
I think of thee in these far happier days,
And thou, my child, from thy bright heaven see
How well I keep my faithful vow to thee.

ELIZABETH GASKELL (1810–1865)

On an Infant dying as soon as born

I saw where in the shroud did lurk
A curious frame of Nature's work;
A floweret crush'd in the bud,
A nameless piece of Babyhood,
Was in her cradle-coffin lying;
Extinct, with scarce the sense of dying:
So soon to exchange the imprisoning womb
For darker closets of the tomb!
She did but ope an eye, and put
A clear beam forth, then straight up shut
For the long dark: ne'er more to see
Through glasses of mortality.
    Riddle of destiny, who can show
What thy short visit meant, or know
What thy errand here below?
Shall we say that Nature blind
Check'd her hand, and changed her mind,
Just when she had exactly wrought
A finish'd pattern without fault?
Could she flag, or could she tire,
Or lack'd she the Promethean fire
(With her nine moon's long workings sicken'd)
That should thy little limbs have quicken'd?
Limbs so firm, they seem'd to assure
Life of health, and days mature:
Woman's self in miniature!
Limbs so fair, they might supply
(Themselves now but cold imagery)
The sculptor to make Beauty by.
Or did the stern-eyed Fate descry
That babe or mother, one must die;

So in mercy left the stock
And cut the branch; to save the shock
Of young years widow'd, and the pain
When single state comes back again
To the lone man who, reft of wife,
Thenceforward drags a maimèd life?
The economy of Heaven is dark,
And wisest clerks have miss'd the mark,
Why human buds, like this, should fall,
More brief than fly ephemeral
That has his day; while shrivell'd crones
Stiffen with age to stocks and stones;
And crabbèd use the conscience sears
In sinners of a hundred years.
   Mother's prattle, mother's kiss,
Baby fond, thou ne'er wilt miss:
Rites, which custom does impose,
Silver bells, and baby clothes;
Coral redder than those lips
Which pale death did late eclipse;
Music framed for infants' glee,
Whistle never tuned for thee;
Though thou want'st not, thou shalt have them,
Loving hearts were they which gave them.
Let not one be missing; nurse,
See them laid upon the hearse
Of infant slain by doom perverse.
Why should kings and nobles have
Pictured trophies to their grave,
And we, churls, to thee deny
Thy pretty toys with thee to lie—
A more harmless vanity?

CHARLES LAMB (1775–1834)

14

Infant Joy

'I have no name: Pretty joy!
'I am but two days old.'   Sweet joy but two days old,
What shall I call thee?   Sweet joy I call thee:
'I happy am,   Thou dost smile,
'Joy is my name.'   I sing the while,
Sweet joy befall thee!   Sweet joy befall thee!

WILLIAM BLAKE (1757–1827)

Empty Cradle

A baby's cradle with no baby in it,
A baby's grave where autumn leaves drop sere;
The sweet soul gathered home to Paradise,
The body waiting here.

CHRISTINA ROSSETTI (1830–1894)

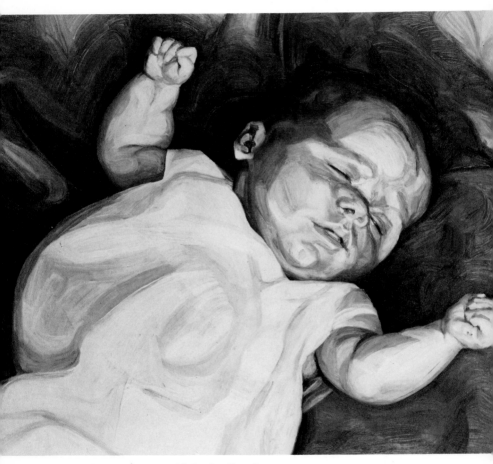

'Baby on a green sofa'. Lucian Freud

Things like Ourselves

from: The Mad Lover

Things like ourselves, as sensual, vain, invented
Bubbles, and breaths of air, got with an itching,
As blisters are and bred; as much corruption
Flows from their lives: sorrow conceives and shapes 'em;
And oftentimes the death of those we love most.
The breeders bring 'em to the world to curse them,
Cares and continual crosses keeping with them.
They make time old to tend them, and experience
An ass: they alter so, they grow, and goodly,
Ere we can turn our thoughts, like drops of water
They fall into the main, and are known no more.

FRANCIS BEAUMONT (1584–1616)
and JOHN FLETCHER (1579–1625)

Child Crying

My daughter cries, and I
Lift her from where she lies,
Carry her here and there,
Talk nonsense endlessly.
And still she cries and cries
In rage, mindlessly.

A trivial anguish, found
In every baby-book.
But, at a fortnight old,
A pink and frantic mound
Of appetites, each look
Scans unfamiliar ground.

A name without a face
Becomes a creature, takes
A creature's energies.
Raging in my embrace.
She takes the world and shakes
Each firm appointed place.

No language blocks her way,
Oblique, loaded with tact.
Hunger and pain are real,
And in her blindness they
Are all she sees: the fact
Is what you cannot say.

Our difference is that
We gauge what each cry says,
Supply what need demands.
Or try to. All falls flat
If cure is wrong or guess
Leaves her still obdurate.

So through uncertainties
I carry her here and there,
And feel her human heart,
Her human miseries,
And in her language share
Her blind and trivial cries.

ANTHONY THWAITE (1930–   )

Baby. *John Constable*

On the Death of a fair Infant

O fairest flower no sooner blown but blasted,
Soft silken Primrose fading timelesslie,
Summers chief honour if thou hadst out-lasted,
Bleak winters force that made thy blossome drie;
For he being amorous on that lovely die
    That did thy cheek envermeil, thought to kiss
But kill'd alas, and then bewayl'd his fatal bliss.

For since grim Aquilo his charioter
By boistrous rape th'Athenian damsel got,
He thought it toucht his Deitie full neer,
If likewise he some fair one wedded not,
Thereby to wipe away th'infamous blot,
    Of long-uncoupled bed, and childless eld,
Which 'mongst the wanton gods a foul reproach was held.

So mounting up in ycie-pearled carr,
Through middle empire of the freezing aire
He wanderd long, till thee he spy'd from farr,
There ended was his quest, there ceast his care.
Down he descended from Snow-soft chaire,
    But all unwares with his cold-kind embrace
Unhous'd thy Virgin Soul from her fair biding place.

Yet art thou not inglorious in thy fate;
For so *Apollo*, with unweeting hand
Whilome did slay his dearly-loved mate
Young *Hyacinth* born on *Eurota's* strand,
Young *Hyacinth* the pride of *Spartan* land;
    But then transform'd him to a purple flower
Alack that so to change thee winter had no power.

Yet can I not perswade me thou art dead
Or that thy coarse corrupts in earths dark wombe,
Or that thy beauties lie in wormie bed,
Hid from the world in a low delved tombe;
Could Heav'n for pittie thee so strictly doom?
    Oh no? for something in thy face did shine
Above mortalitie that shew'd thou wast divine.

Resolve me then oh Soul most surely blest
(If so it be that thou these plaints dost hear)
Tell me bright Spirit where e're thou hoverest
Whether above that high first-moving Spheare
Or in the Elisian fields (if such there were.)
    Oh say me true if thou wert mortal wight
And why from us so quickly thou didst take thy flight.

Wert thou some Starr which from the ruin'd roofe
Of shak't Olympus by mischance didst fall;
Which careful *Jove* in natures true behoofe
Took up, and in fit place did reinstall?
Or did of late earths Sonnes besiege the wall
    Of sheenie Heav'n, and thou some goddess fled
Amongst us here below to hide thy nectar'd head.

Or wert thou that just Maid who once before
Forsook the hated earth, O tell me sooth
And cam'st again to visit us once more?
Or wert thou that sweet smiling Youth?
Or that crown'd Matron sage white-robbed truth?
    Or any other of that heav'nly brood
Let down in clowdie throne to do the world some good.

Or wert thou of the golden-winged hoast,
Who having clad thy self in humane weed,
To earth from thy præfixed seat didst poast,
And after short abode flie back with speed,
As if to shew what creatures Heav'n doth breed,
    Thereby to set the hearts of men on fire
To scorn the sordid world, and unto Heav'n aspire.

Head of a Child.
Rembrandt van Rijn

But oh why didst thou not stay here below
To bless us with thy heav'n-lov'd innocence,
To slake his wrath whom sin hath made our foe
To turn Swift-rushing black perdition hence,
Or drive away the slaughtering pestilence,
   To stand 'twixt us and our deserved smart?
But thou canst best perform that office where thou art.

Then thou the mother of so sweet a child
Her false imagin'd loss cease to lament,
And wisely learn to curb thy sorrows wild;
Think what a present thou to God hast sent,
And render him with patience what he lent;
   This if thou do he will an off-spring give,
That till the worlds last-end shall make thy name to live.

JOHN MILTON (1608–1674)

22

Sephestia's Song to Her Childe

From: Menaphon

Weepe not my wanton! smile upon my knee!
When thou art olde, ther's grief inough for thee!
    Mothers wagge, pretie boy.
    Fathers sorrow, fathers joy.
    When thy father first did see
    Such a boy by him and mee,
    He was glad, I was woe.
    Fortune changde made him so,
    When he left his pretie boy,
    Last his sorowe, first his joy.

Weepe not my wanton! smile upon my knee!
When thou art olde, ther's griefe inough for thee!
    Streaming teares that never stint,
    Like pearle drops from a flint,
    Fell by course from his eyes,
    That one anothers place supplies:
    Thus he grievd in everie part,
    Teares of bloud fell from his hart,
    When he left his pretie boy,
    Fathers sorrow, fathers joy.

Weepe not my wanton! smile upon my knee!
When thou art olde, ther's griefe inough for thee!
    The wanton smilde, father wept;
    Mother cride, babie lept:
    More he crowde, more we cride,
    Nature could not sorowe hide.
    He must goe, he must kisse
    Childe and mother, babie blisse:
    For he left his pretie boy,
    Fathers sorowe, fathers joy.

Weepe not my wanton! smile upon my knee!
When thou art olde, ther's grief inough for thee!

ROBERT GREENE (1558–1592)

On My First Son

Farewell, thou child of my right hand, and joy;
My sin was too much hope of thee, loved boy:
Seven years thou wert lent to me, and I thee pay,
Exacted by thy fate, on the first day.
O, could I lose all father, now! For why
Will man lament the state he should envy?
To have so soon 'scaped world's, and flesh's rage,
And, if no other misery, yet age!
Rest in soft peace, and, ask'd, say here doth lie
BEN. JONSON his best piece of Poetry:
For whose sake, henceforth, all his vows be such,
As what he loves may never like too much.

BEN JONSON (1573?–1637)

Learning to Walk. *Rembrandt van Rijn*

C is for Child

See how her arms now rise and fall,
   See how, like wings, they beat the air:
An arm to balance either foot,
   She moves, half-fluttering, here and there.

And still those motions will suggest
   A different life that's left behind
In early days, remote and strange;
   Felt in that little unformed mind
For one short season, after birth –
Before her feet are claimed by Earth.

W.H. DAVIES (1871–1940)

Characteristics of a Child Three Years Old

Loving she is, and tractable, though wild;
And Innocence hath privilege in her
To dignify arch looks and laughing eyes;
And feats of cunning; and the pretty round
Of trespasses, affected to provoke
Mock-chastisement and partnership in play.
And, as a faggot sparkles on the hearth,
Not less if unattended and alone
Than when both young and old sit gathered round
And take delight in its activity;
Even so this happy Creature of herself
Is all-sufficient, solitude to her
Is blithe society, who fills the air
With gladness and involuntary songs.
Light are her sallies as the tripping fawn's
Forth-startled from the fern where she lay couched;
Unthought-of, unexpected, as the stir
Of the soft breeze ruffling the meadow-flowers,
Or from before it chasing wantonly
The many-coloured images imprest
Upon the bosom of a placid lake.

WILLIAM WORDSWORTH (1770–1850)

A Girl of Three

from: Remembering Golden Bells

Pretty and guileless, – a girl of three.
Not a boy, – but still better than nothing:
To soothe one's feeling, – from time to time a kiss!
There came a day, – they suddenly took her from me;
Her soul's shadow wandered I know not where.
And when I remember how just as the time she died
She lisped strange sounds, beginning to learn to talk,
Then I know that the ties of flesh and blood
Only bind us to a load of grief and sorrow.
At last, by thinking of the time before she was born,
By thought and reason I drove the pain away.
Since my heart forgot her, many days have passed
And three times winter has changed to spring.
This morning, for a little, the old grief came back,
Because, in the road, I met her foster-nurse.

Po Chü-i (772–846)
   translated by Arthur Waley (1889–1966)

'The Woodman's Child' *Arthur Hughes*

On The Death of a little Child

Her pretty dances were her own,
  Her songs were by no other sung;
And all the laughter in her house
  Was started by her own sweet tongue.

This little dance and song composer,
  This laughter maker, sweet and small,
Will never more be seen or heard –
  For her the Sexton's bell does toll.

The shining eyes are closed for aye,
  And that small, crimson mouth of mirth;
The little feet, the little hands –
  All stiff and cold inside the earth.

W.H. DAVIES (1871–1940)

A Child

A child's a plaything for an hour;
   Its pretty tricks we try
For that or for a longer space –
   Then tire, and lay it by.

But I knew one that to itself
   All seasons could control;
That would have mock'd the sense of pain
   Out of a grievèd soul.

Thou straggler into loving arms,
   Young climber-up of knees,
When I forget thy thousand ways
   Then life and all shall cease.

MARY LAMB (1765–1847)

From:

Intimations of Immortality

from Recollections of Early Childhood

Our birth is but a sleep and a forgetting:
The Soul that rises with us, our life's Star,
    Hath had elsewhere its setting,
      And cometh from afar:
    Not in entire forgetfulness,
    And not in utter nakedness,
But trailing clouds of glory do we come
    From God, who is our home:
Heaven lies about us in our infancy!
Shades of the prison-house begin to close
    Upon the growing Boy,
But He beholds the light, and whence it flows,
    He sees it in his joy;
The Youth, who daily farther from the east
    Must travel, still is Nature's Priest,
    And by the vision splendid
    Is on his way attended;
At length the Man perceives it die away,
And fade into the light of common day.

WILLIAM WORDSWORTH (1770–1850)

Four Years Old –
A Nursery Song

One cannot turn a minute,
But mischief – there you're in it,
A-getting at my books, John,
With mighty bustling looks, John;
Or poking at the roses
In midst of which your nose is;
Or climbing on a table,
No matter how unstable,
And turning up your quaint eye
And half-shut teeth with 'Mayn't I?'
Or else you're off at play, John,
Just as you'd be all day, John,
With hat or not, as happens,
And there you dance, and clap hands,
Or on the grass go rolling,
Or plucking flowers, or bowling,
And getting me expenses
With losing balls o'er fences;
And see what flow'rs the weather
Has render'd fit to gather;
And, when we home must jog, you
Shall ride my back, you rogue you.
Your hat adorn'd with fir-leaves,
Horse-chestnut, oak, and vine-leaves;
And so, with green o'erhead, John,
Shall whistle home to bed, John.
– But see, the sun shines brightly;
Come, put your hat on rightly,
And we'll among the bushes,
And hear your friends the thrushes.

LEIGH HUNT (1784–1859)

On Children

How dull our days, how lacking in surprise
Without these small epitomes of sin,
These flowers with their store of life within
And grave, appalling freshness in their eyes.

FRANCES CORNFORD (1886–1960)

Little Girl. *August Edouart*

Child and Mother

from: On Receipt of my Mother's picture out of Norfolk

Where once we dwelt our name is heard no more,
Children not thine have trod my nurs'ry floor;
And where the gard'ner Robin, day by day,
Drew me to school along the public way,
Delighted with my bauble coach, and wrapt
In scarlet mantle warm, and velvet capt,
'Tis now become a history little known,
That once we call'd the past'ral house our own.
Short-liv'd possession! but the record fair
That mem'ry keeps of all thy kindness there,
Still outlives many a storm that has effac'd
A thousand other themes less deeply trac'd.
Thy nightly visits to my chamber made,
That thou might'st know me safe and warmly laid;
Thy morning bounties ere I left my home,
The biscuit, or confectionary plum;
The fragrant waters on my cheeks bestow'd
By thy own hand, till fresh they shone and glow'd:
All this, and more endearing still than all,
Thy constant flow of love, that knew no fall,
Ne'er roughen'd by those cataracts and breaks,
That humour interpos'd too often makes;

All this still legible in mem'ry's page,
And still to be so, to my latest age,
Adds joy to duty, makes me glad to pay
Such honours to thee as my numbers may;
Perhaps a frail memorial, but sincere,
Not scorn'd in heav'n, though little notic'd here.
Could Time, his flight revers'd, restore the hours
When, playing with thy vesture's tissued flow'rs —
The violet, the pink, and jassamine —
I prick'd them into paper with a pin,
(And thou wast happier than myself the while,
Would'st softly speak, and stroke my head, and smile)
Could those few pleasant hours again appear,
Might one wish bring them, would I wish them here?
I would not trust my heart — the dear delight
Seems so to be desir'd, perhaps I might. —
But no: — what here we call our life is such,
So little to be lov'd, and thou so much,
That I should ill requite thee to constrain
Thy unbound spirit into bonds again.

WILLIAM COWPER (1731–1800)

'An Anxious Hour'. *Alexander Farmer*

A Child Ill

Oh, little body, do not die.
    The soul looks out through wide blue eyes
So questioningly into mine,
    That my tormented soul replies:

'Oh, little body, do not die.
    You hold the soul that talks to me
Although our conversation be
    As wordless as the windy sky.'

So looked my father at the last
    Right in my soul, before he died.
Though words we spoke went heedless past
    As London traffic-roar outside.

And now the same blue eyes I see
    Look through me from a little son,
So questioning, so searchingly
    That youthfulness and age are one.

My father looked at me and died
    Before my soul made full reply.
Lord, leave this other Light alight –
    Oh, little body, do not die.

JOHN BETJEMAN (1906–   )

On a Child Beginning to Talk

Methinks 'tis pretty sport to hear a child
Rocking a word in mouth yet undefiled;
The tender racket rudely plays the sound,
Which, weakly bandied, cannot back rebound.
And the soft air the softer roof doth kiss,
With a sweet dying and a pretty miss,
Which hears no answer yet from the white rank
Of teeth, not risen from their coral bank.
The alphabet is searched for letters soft,
To try a word before it can be wrought;
And, when it slideth forth, it goes as nice
As when a man doth walk upon the ice.

THOMAS BASTARD (1566–1618)

Children's Song

We live in our world,
A world that is too small
For you to stoop and enter
Even on hands and knees,
The adult subterfuge.
And though you probe and pry
With analytic eye,
And eavesdrop all our talk
With an amused look,
You cannot find the centre
Where we dance, where we play,
Where life is still asleep
Under the closed flower,
Under the smooth shell
Of eggs in the cupped nest
That mock the faded blue
Of your remoter heaven.

R. S. THOMAS (1915–   )

I Remember, I Remember

I remember, I remember
The house where I was born,
The little window where the sun
Came peeping in at morn;
He never came a wink too soon,
Nor brought too long a day;
But now, I often wish the night
Had borne my breath away!

I remember, I remember
The roses, red and white,
The violets, and the lily-cups,
Those flowers made of light!
The lilacs where the robin built,
And where my brother set
The laburnum on his birthday, –
The tree is living yet!

I remember, I remember
Where I was used to swing,
And thought the air must rush as fresh
To swallows on the wing;
My spirit flew in feathers then,
That is so heavy now,
And summer pools could hardly cool
The fever on my brow!

I remember, I remember
The fir trees dark and high;
I used to think their slender tops
Were close against the sky:
It was a childish ignorance,
But now 'tis little joy
To know I'm farther off from heav'n
Than when I was a boy.

THOMAS HOOD (1799–1845)

Little Boy. *Gwen John*

The Land of Counterpane

When I was sick and lay a-bed,
I had two pillows at my head,
And all my toys beside me lay
To keep me happy all the day.

And sometimes for an hour or so
I watched my leaden soldiers go,
With different uniforms and drills,
Among the bed-clothes, through the hills;

And sometimes sent my ships in fleets
All up and down among the sheets;
Or brought my trees and houses out,
And planted cities all about.

I was the giant great and still
That sits upon the pillow-hill,
And sees before him, dale and plain,
The pleasant land of counterpane.

R.L. STEVENSON (1850–1894)

Children, Children

Children, children,
the dull and the clever
like a tide coming in
for ever and ever.

Children, children
ugly ones and pretty ones
Children, children,
country ones and city ones.

Each of them someone's son or daughter
leaping and shining like restless water
mouths and noses, eyes and ears
ready for laughter, ready for tears:

minds and bodies always moving:
where do they come from? They come from loving.

All those heads
and all those faces
they come from loving
in secret places:

from heat of love
all were begotten:
from love still burning
or love forgotten.

JOHN WAIN (1925–   )

A Cradle Song

Sleep, Sleep, beauty bright
Dreaming o'er the joys of night.
Sleep, Sleep: in thy sleep
Little sorrows sit & weep.

Sweet Babe, in thy face
Soft desires I can trace
Secret joys & secret smiles
Little pretty infant wiles.

As thy softest limbs I feel
Smiles as of the morning steal
O'er thy cheek & o'er thy breast
Where thy little heart does rest.

O, the cunning wiles that creep
In thy little heart asleep.
When thy little heart does wake,
Then the dreadful lightnings break.

From thy cheek & from thy eye
O'er the youthful harvests nigh
Infant wiles & infant smiles
Heaven & Earth of peace beguiles.

WILLIAM BLAKE (1757–1827)

44

'Le berceau'. *Berthe Morisot*

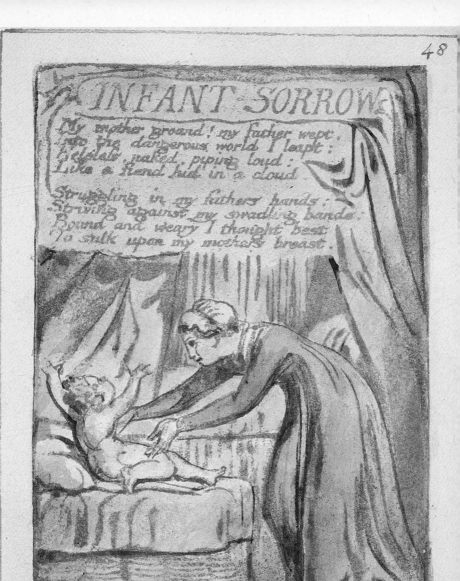

'Infant Sorrow'. *William Blake*

Infant Sorrow

My mother groan'd, my father wept;
Into the dangerous world I leapt,
Helpless, naked, piping loud,
Like a fiend hid in a cloud.

Struggling in my father's hands
Striving against my swaddling bands,
Bound & weary, I thought best
To sulk upon my mother's breast.

When I saw that rage was vain,
And to sulk would nothing gain,
Turning many a trick & wile,
I began to soothe & smile.

And I sooth'd day after day
Till upon the ground I stray;
And I smil'd night after night,
Seeking only for delight.

And I saw before me shine
Clusters of the wand'ring vine,
And many a lovely flower & tree
Stretch'd their blossoms out to me.

WILLIAM BLAKE (1757—1827)

The Hoyden

A Cautionary Tale

Miss Agnes had two or three dolls, and a box
To hold all their bonnets, and tippets, and frocks.
In a red leather thread case, that snapped when it shut
She had needles to sew with, and scissors to cut:
But Agnes lik'd better to play with rude boys
Than work with her needle, or play with her toys;
Young ladies should always appear neat and clean,
Yet Agnes was seldom drest fit to be seen.
I saw her one day attempting to throw
A very large stone when it fell on her toe,
The boys who were present, and saw what was done,
Set up a loud laugh, and call'd it fine fun.
But I took her home, and the doctor soon came,
And Agnes I fear will a long time be lame,
And from morning till night she laments very much,
That now when she walks she must lean on a crutch,
And she has told her dear father a thousand times o'er,
That she never will play with rude boys any more.

ANONYMOUS (1811)

Rhyme for a London Street Game

I am a little beggar-girl,
My mother she is dead,
My father is a drunkard
And won't give me no bread.
I look out of the window
To hear the organ play —
God bless my dear mother,
She gone far away.
Ding-dong the castle bells
Bless my poor mother —
Her coffin shall be black,
Six white angels at her back —
Two to watch and two to pray,
And two to carry her soul away.

ANONYMOUS

Listen to Reason

One afternoon, as Joseph West,
The boy who learned his lesson best,
Was trying how his whip would crack,
By chance hit Headstrong on the back.

Enrag'd he flew, and gave poor Joe,
With all his might, a sudden blow:
Nor would he listen to one word,
When Joe endeavoured to be heard.

Joe finding him resolv'd to fight,
For what was accidental quite,
Although he never fought before,
Beat Headstrong till he'd have no more.

ANONYMOUS (1811)

Thomas Bewick

The Child on the Cliffs

Mother, the root of this little yellow flower
Among the stones has the taste of quinine.
Things are strange to-day on the cliff. The sun shines so
   bright,
And the grasshopper works at his sewing-machine
So hard. Here's one on my hand, mother, look;
I lie so still. There's one on your book.

But I have something to tell more strange. So leave
Your book to the grasshopper, mother dear, –
Like a green knight in a dazzling market-place –
And listen now. Can you hear what I hear
Far out? Now and then the foam there curls
And stretches a white arm out like a girl's.

Fishes and gulls ring no bells. There cannot be
A chapel or church between here and Devon,
With fishes or gulls ringing its bell, – hark! –
Somewhere under the sea or up in heaven.
'It's the bell, my son, out in the bay
On the buoy. It does sound sweet to-day.'

Sweeter I never heard, mother, no, not in all Wales.
I should like to be lying under that foam,
Dead, but able to hear the sound of the bell,
And certain that you would often come
And rest, listening happily.
I should be happy if that could be.

EDWARD THOMAS (1878–1917)

Seven Yere of Age

(in the Middle Ages)

Aha, Wanton is my name!
I can many a quaynte game.
Lo, my toppe I dryve in same,
Se, it torneth rounde!
I can with my scorge-stycke
My felowe upon the heed hytte,
And lyghtly from hym make a skyppe;
And blere on hym my tonge.
If brother or syster do me chyde
I wyll scratche and also byte.
I can crye, and also kyke,
And mock them all berewe.
If fader or mother wyll me smyte,
I wyll wrynge with my lyppe;
And lyghtly from hym make a skyppe;
And call my dame shrewe.
Aha, a newe game have I founde:
Se this gynne it renneth rounde;
And here another have I founde,
And yet mo can I fynde.
I can mowe on a man;
And make a lesynge well I can,
And mayntayne it ryte well than.
This connynge came me of kynde.
Ye, syrs, I can well gelde a snayle;
And catche a coew by the tayle;
This is a fayre connynge!

John Selwyn's Children. *From a memorial brass*

I can daunce, and also skyppe;
I can playe at the chery pytte;
And I can wystell you a fytte,
Syres, in a whylowe ryne.
Ye, syrs, and every day
Whan I to scole shall take the waye
Some good mannes gardyn I wyll assaye,
Perys and plommes to plucke.
I can spye a sparowes nest.
I wyll not go to scole but whan me lest,
For there begynneth a sory fest
Whan the mayster sholde lyfte my docke.
But syrs, what I was seven yere of age,
I was sent to the Worlde to take wage.
And this seven yere I have been his page
And kept his commaundment : . .

A N O N Y M O U S

Thomas Bewick

The Poet at ten years old
from: The Prelude

Fair seed-time had my soul, and I grew up
Fostered alike by beauty and by fear:
Much favoured in my birth-place, and no less
In that belovèd Vale to which erelong
We were transplanted; – there were we let loose
For sports of wider range. Ere I had told
Ten birth-days, when among the mountain slopes
Frost, and the breath of frosty wind, had snapped
The last autumnal crocus, 'twas my joy
With store of springes o'er my shoulder hung
To range the open heights where woodcocks run
Along the smooth green turf. Through half the night,

Scudding away from snare to snare, I plied
That anxious visitation; – moon and stars
Were shining o'er my head. I was alone,
And seemed to be a trouble to the peace
That dwelt among them. Sometimes it befell
In these night wanderings, that a strong desire
O'erpowered my better reason, and the bird
Which was the captive of another's toil
Became my prey; and when the deed was done
I heard among the solitary hills
Low breathings coming after me, and sounds
Of undistinguishable motion, steps,
Almost as silent as the turf they trod.

WILLIAM WORDSWORTH (1770–1850)

Thomas Bewick

Ballroom Dancing Class

The little girls' frocks are frilly.
   The little boys' suits are blue.
On little gold chairs
They perch in pairs
   Awaiting their Friday cue.
The little boys stamp like ponies.
   The little girls coo like doves.
The little boys pummel their cronies
   With white, enormous gloves.
And overhead from a balcony
The twittering mothers crane to see.

Though sleek the curls
Of the little girls,
   Tossing their locks like foam,
Each little boy's tie
Has slipped awry
   And his hair forgets the comb.
He harks to the tuning fiddle
   With supercilious sneers.
His voice is cracked in the middle,
   Peculiar are his ears.
And little girls' mothers nod with poise
To distracted mothers of little boys.

'Little Rose of Lyme Regis'. *J A McN Whistler*

57

Curtsying to the hostess,
  The little girls dip in line.
But hobbledehoy
Bobs each little boy,
  And a ramrod is his spine.
With little girls' charms prevailing,
  Why, as the music starts,
Are the little girls' mothers paling?
  And why do they clasp their hearts
When the hostess says with an arching glance,
'Let boys choose partners before we dance'?

Now little girls sway
Like buds in May
  And tremble upon the stalk.
But little boys wear
An arrogant air
  And they swagger when they walk.
The meagerest boy grows taller.
  The shyest one's done with doubt,
As he fingers a manful collar
  And singles his charmer out,
Or rakes the circle with narrowed eyes
To choose his suitable Friday prize.
While overhead in the balcony
The little boys' mothers smile to see
On razorless cheek and beardless chin
The Lord-of-Creation look begin.

Oh, little boys beckon, little girls bend!
And little boys' mothers condescend
(As they straighten their furs and pat their pearls)
To nod to the mothers of the little girls.

PHYLLIS MCGINLEY (1905–1978)

Of the Boy and his Top

A little boy had bought a Top,
The best in all the toyman's shop;
He made a whip with good eel's-skin,
He lash'd the top, and made it spin;
All the children within call,
And the servants, one and all,
Stood round to see it and admire.
At last the Top began to tire,
He cried out, 'Pray don't whip me, Master,
You whip too hard, – I can't spin faster,
I can spin quite as well without it.'
The little Boy replied, 'I doubt it;
I only whip you for your good,
You were a foolish lump of wood,
By dint of whipping you were raised
To see yourself admired and praised,
And I left you, you'd remain
A foolish lump of wood again.'

Explanation
Whipping sounds a little odd,
It don't mean whipping with a rod,
It means to teach a boy incessantly,
Whether by lessons or more pleasantly,
Every hour and every day,
By every means, in every way,
By reading, writing, rhyming, talking,
By riding to see sights, and walking:
If you leave off he drops at once,
A lumpish, wooden-headed dunce.

JOHN HOOKHAM FRERE (1796–1846)

Arthur: Constance's Lament

from: The Life and Death of King John

Grief fills the room up of my absent child,
Lies in his bed, walks up and down with me,
Puts on his pretty looks, repeats. his words,
Remembers me of all his gracious parts,
Stuffs out his vacant garments with his form;
Then have I reason to be fond of grief.
Fare you well: had you such a loss as I,
I could give better comfort than you do.
I will not keep this form upon my head,
When there is such disorder in my wit.
O Lord! my boy, my Arthur, my fair son!
My life, my joy, my food, my all the world!
My widow-comfort, and my sorrows' cure!

WILLIAM SHAKESPEARE (1564–1616)

A Child of a Noble Family. *Attributed to Robert Peake*

There Was a Child Went Forth

There was a child went forth every day,
And the first object he look'd upon, that object he became,
And that object became part of him for the day or a certain
   part of the day,
Or for many years or stretching cycles of years.

The early lilacs became part of this child,
And grass and white and red morning-glories, and white
   and red clover, and the song of the phœbe-bird,
And the Third-month lambs and the sow's pink-faint litter,
   and the mare's foal and the cow's calf,
And the noisy brood of the barnyard or by the mire of the
   pond-side,
And the fish suspending themselves so curiously below
   there, and the beautiful curious liquid,
And the water-plants, with their graceful flat heads, all
   became part of him.

WALT WHITMAN (1819–1892)

'The Artist's Daughters'. *Thomas Gainsborough*

'The Mackinnon Children'. *William Hogarth*

What Benefit can Children be?

from: Wit without Money

What benefit can children be
But charges and disobedience? What's the
Love they render at one and twenty years?
I pray die, father. When they are young, they
Are like bells rung backwards, nothing but noise
And giddiness; and come to years once, there
Drops a son by the sword in his mistress's
Quarrel, a great joy to his parents: a
Daughter ripe too, grows high and lusty in
Her blood, runs away
With a supple-hamm'd serving man, his twenty
Nobles spent, takes to a trade, and learns to spin.

FRANCIS BEAUMONT (1584–1616)
and JOHN FLETCHER (1579–1625)

Dirty Jim

There was one little Jim
'Tis reported of him,
   And must be, to his lasting disgrace,
That he never was seen
With his hands at all clean
   Nor yet ever clean with his face.

His friends were much hurt
To see so much dirt,
   And often they made him quite clean;
But all was in vain,
He was dirty again,
   And not at all fit to be seen.

When to wash he was sent,
He reluctantly went,
   With water to splash himself o'er.
But he seldom was seen
To have wash'd himself clean,
   And often looked worse than before.

The idle and bad,
Like this little lad,
   May be dirty and black, to be sure;
But good boys are seen,
To be decent and clean,
   Altho' they are ever so poor.

JANE TAYLOR (1783–1824)

My Parents Kept Me from Children who were Rough

My parents kept me from children who were rough
Who threw words like stones and who wore torn clothes.
Their thighs showed through rags. They ran in the street
And climbed cliffs and stripped by the country streams.

I feared more than tigers their muscles like iron
Their jerking hands and their knees tight on my arms.
I feared the salt coarse pointing of those boys
Who copied my lisp behind me on the road.

They were lithe, they sprang out behind hedges
Like dogs to bark at my world. They threw mud
While I looked the other way, pretending to smile.
I longed to forgive them, but they never smiled.

STEPHEN SPENDER (1909–   )

'Children Playing'. *Myles Birket Foster*

The Schoolboy

I love to rise in a summer morn
When the birds sing on every tree;
The distant huntsman winds his horn,
And the sky-lark sings with me.
O! what sweet company.

But to go to school in a summer morn,
O! it drives all joy away;
Under a cruel eye outworn,
The little ones spend the day
In sighing and dismay.

Ah! then at times I drooping sit,
And spend many an anxious hour,
Nor in my book can I take delight,
Nor sit in learning's bower,
Worn thro' with the dreary shower.

How can the bird that is born for joy
Sit in a cage and sing?
How can a child, when fears annoy,
But droop his tender wing,
And forget his youthful spring?

O! father & mother, if buds are nip'd
And blossoms blown away,
And if the tender plants are strip'd
Of their joy in the springing day,
By sorrow and care's dismay,

'Going into School'. *Thomas Webster*

How shall the summer arise in joy,
Or the summer fruits appear?
Or how shall we gather what griefs destroy,
Or bless the mellowing year,
When the blasts of winter appear?

WILLIAM BLAKE (1757–1827)

A Medieval Schoolboy's Complaint

Hay, hay, by this day,
What availeth it me though I say nay?

I wold fain be a clerk,
But yet it is a stronge werk;
The birchen twigges be so sharp
It maketh me have a faint hert.
    What availeth it me though I say nay?

On Monday in the morning when I shall rise,
At six of the clok, it is the gise
To go to scole without avise –
I had lever go twenty mile twise.
    What availeth it me though I say nay?

My master looketh as he were mad:
'Where has thou be, thou sory lad?'
'Milke dukkes my moder bad' –
It was no mervaile though I were sad.
    What availeth it me though I say nay?

My master pepered my ars with well good spede;
It was worse than finkell sede;
He wold not leve till it did blede –
Mich sorow have he for his dede!
    What availeth it me though I say nay?

I wold my master were a watt,
And my book a wild catt,
And a brace of grehoundes in his topp:
I wold be glad for to see that!
    What availeth it me though I say nay?

I wold my master were an hare,
And all his bookes houndes were,
And I myself a joly huntère;
To blow my horn I wold not spare,
For if he were dede I wold not care.
    What availeth it me though I say nay?

ANONYMOUS

from:

On a Distant Prospect of Eton College

Say, father Thames, for thou has seen
   Full many a sprightly race
Disporting on thy margent green,
   The paths of pleasure trace;
Who foremost now delight to cleave,
With pliant arm, thy glassy wave?
   The captive linnet which enthral?
What idle progeny succeed
To chase the rolling circle's speed,
   Or urge the flying ball?

While some on earnest business bent
   Their murm'ring labours ply
'Gainst graver hours that bring constraint
   To sweeten liberty:
Some bold adventurers disdain
The limits of their little reign,
   And unknown regions dare descry:
Still as they run they look behind,
They hear a voice in every wind,
   And snatch a fearful joy.

Gay hope is theirs by fancy fed,
   Less pleasing when possest;
The tear forgot as soon as shed,
   The sunshine of the breast:
Theirs buxom health, of rosy hue,
Wild wit, invention ever new,
   And lively cheer, of vigour born;
The thoughtless day, the easy night,
The spirits pure, the slumbers light,
   That fly th' approach of morn.

Eton Boys in Montem Dress. *Rev M W Peters*

Alas! regardless of their doom
  The little victims play;
No sense have they of ills to come,
  Nor care beyond to-day:
Yet see, how all around 'em wait
The ministers of human fate,
  And black Misfortune's baleful train!
Ah, show them where in ambush stand,
To seize their prey, the murth'rous band!
  Ah, tell them, they are men!

THOMAS GRAY (1716–1771)

from:

Upon the Disobedient Child

Children become, while little, our delights!
When they become bigger they begin to fright's.
Their sinful nature prompts them to rebel,
And to delight in paths that lead to hell.
Their parents' love and care they overlook,
As if relation had them quite forsook.
They take the counsel of the wanton's, rather
Than the most grave instruction of a father.
They reckon parents ought to do for them,
Though they the fifth commandment do contemn;
They snap and snarl if parents them control,
Though but in things most hurtful to the soul.
They reckon they are masters, and that we
Who parents are, should to them subjects be!
If parents fain would have a hand in choosing,
The children will have a heart will in refusing.
They'll by wrong doings, under parents gather,
And say it is no sin to rob a father.
They'll jostle parents out of place and power,
They'll make themselves the head and them devour.
How many children, by becoming head,
Have brought their parents to a piece of bread!
Thus they who, at the first, were parents' joy,
Turn that to bitterness, themselves destroy.

JOHN BUNYAN (1628–1688)

There Was a Boy

There was a Boy; ye knew him well, ye cliffs
And islands of Winander! – many a time,
At evening, when the earliest stars began
To move along the edges of the hills,
Rising or setting, would he stand alone,
Beneath the trees, or by the glimmering lake;
And there, with fingers interwoven, both hands
Pressed closely palm to palm and to his mouth
Uplifted, he, as through an instrument,
Blew mimic hootings to the silent owls,
That they might answer him. – And they would shout
Across the watery vale, and shout again,
Responsive to his call, – with quivering peals,
And long halloos, and screams, and echoes loud
Redoubled and redoubled; concourse wild
Of jocund din! And, when there came a pause
Of silence such as baffled his best skill:
Then, sometimes, in that silence, while he hung
Listening, a gentle shock of mild surprise
Has carried far into his heart the voice
Of mountain-torrents; or the visible scene
Would enter unawares into his mind
With all its solemn imagery, its rocks,
Its woods, and that uncertain heaven received
Into the bosom of the steady lake.

WILLIAM WORDSWORTH (1770–1850)

'Snap the Whip'. *Winslow Homer*

At School

from: A Boy's Poem

When but a trembling wind-flower of a child,
They set me in a large and crowded school.
The pale preceptor clad in rusty black,
The reading classes, and the murmuring forms
Were torture; and the ringing playground, hell.
I shrank from crowds of loud and boisterous boys.
The pain and forfeit of each game was mine;
Contempt, and scorn, and taunts were rained on me;
I wept within my little bed at night,
And wished that I were happy in my grave.
From out this depth of sorrow, slowly grew
A kindred and strange sympathy with eve,
With the unhoused and outcast winds, and with
The rain which I had heard so often weep
Alone, within the middle of the night,
Like a poor, beaten, and despisèd child
That has been thrust forth from its father's door.

ALEXANDER SMITH (1829–1867)

From a Regency-period illustration

'The Fight Interrupted'. *William Mulready*

A Fight at School

from: A Boy's Poem

Upon a day of wind and heavy rain
A crowd was huddling in the porch at school:
As I came up I heard a voice cry out,
'Ho, ho! here comes the lad that talks with ghosts
Sitting upon the graves.' They laughed and jeered,
And gathered round me in a mocking ring,
And hurt me with their faces and their eyes.
With bitter words I smote them in my hate,
As with a weapon. A sudden blow, and wrath
Sprang upward like a flame. I struck, and blood,
Brighter than rubies, gleamed upon my hand;
And at the beauteous sight, from head to heel
A tiger's joy ran tingling through my veins,
And every finger hungered for a throat.
I burst the broken ring, and darted off
With my blood boiling, and my pulses mad.
I did not feel the rain upon my face;
With burning mouth I drank the cooling wind; –
And then, as if my limbs were touched by death,
A shudder shook me, all the rage that sprang
Like sudden fire in a deserted house
Making the windows fierce, had passed away;
And the cold rain beat heavy on me now;
The winds went through me.

ALEXANDER SMITH (1829–1867)

American Boy

from: The Lost World

       I wash my hands, Pop gives his pay
Envelope to Mama; we sit down to our meal.
The phone rings: Mrs Mercer wonders if I'd care
To go to the library. That would be ideal,
I say when Mama lets me. I comb my hair
And find the four books I have out: *The Food
Of the Gods* was best. Liking that world where
The children eat, and grow giant and good,
I swear as I've often sworn: '*I'll* never forget
What it's like, when *I've* grown up.' A prelude
By Chopin, hammered note by note, like alphabet
Blocks, comes from next door. It's played with real feeling,
The feeling of being indoors practicing. 'And yet
It's not as if — ' a gray electric, stealing
To the curb on silent wheels, has come; and I
See on the back seat (sight more appealing
Than any human sight!) my own friend Lucky,

Half wolf, half police-dog. And he can play the piano –
Play that he does, that is – and jump so high
For a ball that he turns a somersault. 'Hello,'
I say to the lady, and hug Lucky . . . In my
Talk with the world, in which it tells me what I know
And I tell it, 'I know – ' how strange that I
Know nothing, and yet it tells me what I know! –
I appreciate the animals, who stand by
Purring. Or else they sit and pant. It's so –
So *agreeable*. If only people purred and panted!
So, now, Lucky and I sit in our row,
Mrs Mercer in hers. I take for granted
The tiller by which she steers, the yellow roses
In the bud vases, the whole enchanted
Drawing room of our progress. The glass encloses
As glass does, a womanish and childish
And doggish universe. We press our noses
To the glass and wish: the angel- and devilfish
Floating by on Vine, on Sunset, shut their eyes
And press their noses to their glass and wish.

RANDALL JARRELL (1914–1965)

85

'The Romps'. *W R Bigg*

'The Masters Gawler'. *Sir Joshua Reynolds*

Floreat Etona

from: School and Schoolfellows

Twelve years ago I made a mock
    Of filthy trades and traffics:
I wondered what they meant by stock;
    I wrote delightful sapphics;
I knew the streets of Rome and Troy,
    I supped with Fates and Furies, –
Twelve years ago I was a boy,
    A happy boy, at Drury's.

Twelve years ago! – how many a thought
    Of faded pains and pleasures
Those whispered syllables have brought
    From Memory's hoarded treasures!
The fields, the farms, the bats, the books,
    The glories and disgraces,
The voices of dear friends, the looks
    Of old familiar faces!

Kind Mater smiles again to me,
    As bright as when we parted;
I seem again the frank, the free,
    Stout-limbed, and simple-hearted!
Pursuing every idle dream,
    And shunning every warning;
With no hard work but Bovney stream,
    No chill except Long Morning:

Now stopping Harry Vernon's ball
    That rattled like a rocket;
Now hearing Wentworth's 'Fourteen all!'
    And striking for the pocket;
Now feasting on a cheese and flitch, –
    Now drinking from the pewter;
Now leaping over Chalvey ditch,
    Now laughing at my tutor.

WINTHROP MACKWORTH PRAED (1802–1839)

Mother and Child. *Mary Cassatt*

Index

The names of poets are printed in Roman type, those of artists in *Italics*

Acknowledgments

The editor and publishers would like to thank the following for permission
to reproduce certain copyright poems:

John Betjeman, *A Child Ill* from COLLECTED POEMS: John Murray Ltd

Frances Cornford, *On Children* from COLLECTED POEMS: Cresset Press

W.H. Davies, *C is for Child* and *On the Death of a Little Child* from THE
COMPLETE POEMS OF W.H. DAVIES: The Executors of the W.H. Davies
Estate and Jonathan Cape Ltd

Randall Jarrell, *American Boy* from THE LOST WORLD: Eyre & Spottiswode
(Publishers) Ltd

Phyllis McGinley, *Ballroom Dancing Class*: Viking Penguin Inc

Stephen Spender, *My Parents Kept Me from Children who were Rough* from
COLLECTED POEMS by Stephen Spender: reprinted by permission of Faber
and Faber Ltd

R. S. Thomas, *Children's Song* from SELECTED POEMS 1946–68: Granada
Publishing Ltd

Anthony Thwaite, *Child Crying* from THE LESS DECEIVED: The Marvell
Press

John Wain, *Children, Children* from PROFESSING POETRY by John Wain:
Macmillan Ltd

Arthur Waley, translation of *A Girl of Three* by Po Chü-i from ONE
HUNDRED AND SEVENTY CHINESE POEMS: Constable and Co Ltd

While the editor and publishers have made every effort to obtain permission
from the copyright holders of the poems and illustrations in this book, they
would be most grateful to learn of any instances where an incomplete or
incorrect acknowledgment has been made.

'Knucklebones'. *J Wilson Steer*